THREE RULES
FOR LIVING A
GOOD LIFE

"Few souls I've ever encountered had the ability to capture a mind and heart like Coach Lou Holtz. He is as funny as he is inspiring and as wise as he is blunt and honest. Coach is not only the guy you want to invite to the party, he's also the guy you want to be your grandfather. In his newest book, *Three Rules for Living a Good Life*, Lou Holtz delivers timeless and practical paternal wisdom—once again—in a way only he can. As a reader, I was completely engaged with the turn of each page. As a football fanatic, I was enthralled with every story and anecdote; as a Catholic Christian, I was affirmed and challenged to live a more virtuous life. This book is great not only for the young but also for the young at heart. Within these pages are the blueprint for success in faith, life, and love."

Mark Hart
Executive vice president of Life Teen International

"Everyone can benefit from having a mentor, a coach to help them navigate through the stages of life. Coach Lou Holtz shares with the reader his faith-based game plan for life that we were blessed to have him present to Franciscan University of Steubenville's 2015 graduating class. Simple, yet profound, Holtz's game plan is one that everyone who desires to excel in living a good life should consider."

Rev. Sean O. Sheridan, T.O.R.
President of Franciscan University of Steubenville

"I love Lou's theory for winning in the game of life! Lou presents his philosophy and game plan to help a person become a success in life. A great read. Truly AWESOME BABY with a CAPITAL A!"

Dick Vitale
ESPN College Basketball Analyst

"There is no one more qualified to offer advice to young (and not-so-young) people than Coach Holtz. He has lived through life's ups and downs with humor, integrity, and faith. His words inspire me daily, and I will be buying this book for every graduate I know!"

Haley Scott DeMaria
Author, speaker, and member of Notre Dame swimming (1995)

"Lou Holtz is masterful in teaching life lessons that everyone can learn from. A wonderful, witty, easy read that will change your life for the better."

Muffet McGraw
Head coach of the University of Notre Dame Women's Basketball team

"This is another championship book from Lou Holtz. *Three Rules for Living a Good Life* offers incredible and meaningful insights for all graduates (high school, college, and post-graduate) that will help these young women and men navigate successfully through the rest of their lives."

Skip Strzelecki
President of St. Andrews Products

"Lou Holtz made his three rules for living a good life personal and relevant to our employees at Paychex. He inspired them to follow his rules in both their personal and professional lives."

Martin Mucci
President and CEO of Paychex, Inc.

"Lou Holtz is an incredibly engaging speaker and audiences hang on his every word. Between the amazing challenges and life lessons he's learned and the stories of his family, players, and colleagues, he relates everything back to the audience. Everyone who hears Lou walks away with his encouraging words and the energy and enthusiasm to be a better person."

Nika Spencer
Senior event manager at the Washington Speakers Bureau

"Coach Holtz is incredible. He is personable and genuine, and he had our entire audience captivated. An overwhelming number of our attendees reached out to us after our event to comment about how much they loved his keynote!"

Julia TenHoeve
Senior marketing associate at a global financial service firm

THREE RULES
FOR LIVING A
GOOD LIFE

A Game Plan for after Graduation

LOU HOLTZ

AVE MARIA PRESS AVE Notre Dame, Indiana

© 2019 by Lou Holtz

All rights reserved. No part of this book may be used or reproduced in any manner whatsoever, except in the case of reprints in the context of reviews, without written permission from Ave Maria Press®, Inc., P.O. Box 428, Notre Dame, IN 46556, 1-800-282-1865.

Founded in 1865, Ave Maria Press is a ministry of the United States Province of Holy Cross.

www.avemariapress.com

Hardcover: ISBN-13 978-1-59471-906-6

E-book: ISBN-13 978-1-59471-907-3

Cover image courtesy of Kevin R. Cooke.

Cover and text design by Brian C. Conley.

Printed and bound in the United States of America.

Library of Congress Cataloging-in-Publication Data is available.

CONTENTS

WELCOME TO YOUR NEW LIFE

Congratulations on the conclusion of your school days and for beginning the next stage of your life.

Long ago, I graduated from college too. In fact, I happened to be in the lower one-third of my class. If it weren't for people like me there would have been no upper tier of the class!

I'm going to make five assumptions about some goals you have for your life right now. I'm going to guess that you want these things:

1. You want to be successful professionally.
2. You want to have a good personal life.
3. You want to feel you are needed.
4. You want to feel secure about your future.
5. You want to go to heaven.

The good news is that all of these are reachable goals. In this book I'm going to give you a simple plan to achieve your goals in all of these areas. And they all work together. You won't have to sacrifice your personal life or your religious practices and beliefs in order to advance professionally. It really is a simple plan. Just don't complicate it.

Personally, I always try to keep things simple in my life. I often think of it this way: Do you realize that there are only seven colors of the rainbow? But look what Michelangelo did with those seven colors. There are only seven musical notes in a scale too. But look at what Beethoven did with those seven notes.

These artists didn't complicate things. They kept it simple. You can do the same.

In this book, I'm not going to preach to you. I'm not going to lecture to you. I'm going to tell you about things I believe and the experiences I have had. I'm not going to tell you about things I've read about or heard about. I'm only going to tell you about things that I believe. And let me tell you why you might want to listen to me, Lou Holtz, the former football coach and ESPN analyst: I have been your age, whether you are twenty-one, or twenty-five, or even eighteen. But most of you have not lived in your ninth decade like me!

A Message of Faith

Another assumption I can make about you is that you want to be happy. Happiness comes in many forms:

- If you want to be happy for an hour, eat a steak.
- If you want to be happy for a day, play golf.
- If you want to be happy for a week, go on a cruise. (I say this while admitting that being on a cruise is

a lot like being in jail, except you have a chance to drown.)

- If you want to be happy for a month, buy a new car.
- If you want to be happy for a year, win the lottery.

At the Last Supper, Jesus said, "I am the way and the truth and the life." So if you truly want to be happy for a lifetime, put your faith in Jesus Christ. I have a strong faith in Jesus Christ, and I don't know how I could live without him.

I hope you will appreciate how very fortunate you are to have the freedom to live in a place where you can believe in God and have the freedom to be able to share your faith with others.

At this stage of life, your willingness to practice your faith may be at a crossroads. Lately, maybe you have stopped going to church on Sunday as often as you should. Maybe you have quit praying altogether. You have a newfound independence. You may have a greater tendency to want to do things on your own.

Just always remember the old saying "If you want to make God laugh, just tell him what your plans are."

Personally, I don't know how people live without constant prayer. When I was coaching, I can't tell you how many I times I prayed when Michigan had the ball on our four-yard line. "O, God, you stop them from scoring and I am going to change my life."

If you truly want to be happy for a lifetime, put your faith in Jesus Christ.

It's like the businessman who was late for an important meeting. He kept circling around the parking lot for minutes without finding a place to park his car. So he prayed, "God, if you find me a parking place I'll go to church every Sunday the rest of my life. And I will not drink alcohol ever again." Just then, miraculously, a parking spot opened up. And the man looked up to heaven and said, "Forget it, God, I found one on my own."

Don't ignore God! Don't give up your faith!

What You Need for Your Life

With your school years being complete, you are looking for something new to do. Lots of this search will involve finding a professional career. You may be looking for someone to love. Everybody needs someone to love. You also need someone to believe in. For me, that *someone* is Jesus Christ, my Lord and Savior.

You need one more thing. You need something to hope for. Having hopes, dreams, and ambitions are absolutely critical.

In this regard, don't make the same mistake that I made. Everyone does dumb things, but there is one thing in particular I regret. My coaching staff and I went to the University of Notre Dame in 1986. We found a program at the bottom, and we took it to the very top. And for nine straight years we went to a January 1 bowl game: the Sugar, the Cotton, the Orange, or the Fiesta Bowl. Nobody had done that before, and nobody has done that since. We put our program on top and we *maintained* it. That's the thing I regret the most, the maintenance. You see, there's a fact in life: you are either growing or you are dying. Trees are either growing or dying. So is the grass. So is a marriage. So is a business. So is a person. And this is a fact that doesn't have anything to do with age. It's certainly true for me. My birthday candles cost more than the cake. It's also true for you.

When you are only operating out of maintenance, you are not trying to improve, not trying to get better. At Notre Dame, we got on top and said, "Hey, we got this pretty good. Let's maintain it. Let's not take any risks." But maintenance of our spot on top didn't work. When we finished second at Notre Dame, everyone called me an idiot, even though that didn't seem fair. They call the person who finishes last in medical school "doctor" after all.

Everyone needs bigger dreams. Everyone needs to have something more to hope for.

When I left Notre Dame at age fifty-nine, I didn't think I would coach again. Where do you go after you coach at Notre Dame? According to my mother you go directly to heaven and sit right next to the pope. You certainly don't coach anymore after Notre Dame.

And then I went to live in a town where the average age was deceased. And what I found out was that I wasn't tired of coaching. I needed something to hope for, something to dream. Even though you have already done great things in your life, such as graduate from college, you have to ask, What's going to happen now?

Everyone needs bigger dreams.
Everyone needs to have something
more to hope for.

In the following chapters of this short book I'm going to give you a plan you can apply to reaching those five goals I assumed you have for your life. It's a simple plan. It's one that works. It's a plan I wish I had had for myself when I was your age.

This plan has only three rules you have to follow. Let's take a look at them.

DO WHAT IS RIGHT

Let me put it this way: There is never a right time to do the wrong thing. And there is never a wrong time to do the right thing. The first step of your plan is to do what is right.

How do you know what is right? The answer is one you have heard many times. It comes directly from the Bible. Jesus said, "Do to others whatever you would have them do to you."

This makes a lot of sense. You wouldn't want someone to take something from you without your permission. I once had a player who told me he had found his teammate's wallet before he lost it. "Son, that's called stealing," I had to remind him. So do the same. Don't take something from someone else that is

---

"Do to others whatever you would have them do to you." (Matthew 7:12)

---

not yours. Don't borrow someone else's original idea. Don't cut corners on an assignment your supervisor gives to you. Treat the other person as you want to be treated. It's simple.

And for starters, you can do what is right each day by being honest. Let your yes mean yes and your no mean no. You want others to be truthful with you. You do the same.

Doing What Is Right on a Daily Basis

My long-range goal in coaching football was to advance my career as coach at the highest levels of the sport. To reach my goal, I had to do what was right in decisions big and small. Sometimes this was difficult. Sometimes doing what was right seemed to take me away from my long-range goal. But still, I kept to the plan.

The best I can relate this lesson is through something that happened to me when I was hired to be the head coach at the College of William and Mary in 1969. I was hired by an outstanding school president, Davis Y. Paschall. His direction to me was that he wanted to build a football program that could compete with and eventually join the Atlantic Coast Conference as the conference's eighth member. This could only happen if we had success on the football field.

In our second year, we went to what is now the Citrus Bowl in Orlando. We lost the game to Toledo, the twelfth-ranked team in the country. We continued to progress in the next season, even though we played such teams as West Virginia, North Carolina, and Wake Forest. We were doing a nice job and well underway to building a good, solid program. However, in 1971, Davis Y. Paschall got sick and had to resign. The school hired a new president whose ambition was different. He wanted to deemphasize football and establish more of an Ivy League–type program. I knew I was going to have to leave William and Mary if I was going to achieve my goals and aspirations of being the head football coach of an excellent football program.

During the summer of 1971, just before the season, I received a letter from representatives of North Carolina State informing me that Earle Edwards, their head coach of many years, was retiring and would be replaced with an interim coach until they could hire a full-time coach. They asked me if I was interested in the job. I replied that I was very much interested but would not talk to them about the job until after our season was over. I had an obligation to our football players at William and Mary. They said that was fine.

We started our season and won our first four games. We beat Tulane on their home field in New Orleans. When I arrived home after that game, the North

Carolina State represen-
tatives called again and
said they would like to
interview me immedi-
ately. They said they
wanted to resolve their
head coaching position
before the first Saturday
in December, the day
football recruits could
sign their ACC letters
of intent. I politely in-

photo credit NC State Athletics

formed him that an interview in the coming days
would not be possible because of the obligation I had
to William and Mary. I told them again that if they
wanted to talk to me at the end of the season, I would
love to do so.

They said they were sorry and that they would
move on without me. They told me I would no longer
be a candidate for the North Carolina State job.

Our William and Mary team continued to have a pretty good season. Late in the year we went to play the University of North Carolina at Chapel Hill. They had a great defense, one of the best in the country. Our starting quarterback, Steve Regan, was injured, and we would have to go with our backup, John Gargano, who stood only five foot eight. We did have an excellent wide receiver, David Knight, and we came up with a great game plan for North Carolina.

We went down to Chapel Hill and played an outstanding game. As a matter of fact, we were never behind the entire game and never ahead by more than seven points. With about two minutes left in the game, we led 35–28. North Carolina had the ball at its own twenty-yard line. A third down and ten yards to go play would decide the game. Their left-handed quarterback was Paul Miller. He went back to pass, couldn't find anybody open, and started to scramble. We put pressure on Miller and just before he was hit, he threw the ball down the field. The ball landed on the ground right in front of me at the fifty-yard line and bounced twice.

The official from our conference who could see the play perfectly called it an incomplete pass. But the back judge from the home Atlantic Coast Conference (ACC) came running up and said the pass was completed. So, there was a mixed ruling. The final decision would be made by the referee. He was also from the ACC. He decided to side with the back judge who could not even see the play and ruled it North Carolina's ball on the fifty-yard line. I then got two fifteen-yard unsportsmanlike penalties without ever using one word of profanity. That is hard to do. Two unsportsmanlike penalties for one play. Consequently, North Carolina went from their own twenty-yard line to our twenty-yard line on an incomplete pass.

They scored a touchdown with less than a minute to go and went for the two-point conversion. We deflected the pass, but their receiver, Lewis Jolley, caught it and we lost 36–35. I was devastated, but we had played a great game on the road against a very good team.

We returned home, and I no sooner walked in the door and the phone was ringing. It was the athletic director from North Carolina State. You have to realize that the University of North Carolina was North Carolina State's biggest rival. The NC State athletic director and everybody else were aware of the great performance our team had put on that day. He asked me if I would just visit with him for thirty minutes so he could let me know what the job at his school entailed. Then, if I was interested, they would wait until the end of the season to talk to me again.

I agreed to meet with him for thirty minutes, and I became more convinced that NC State would be a good place to further my coaching career.

A few weeks later, right before our last game, the Quarterback Club of William and Mary supporters invited me to their meeting and presented me with a new car. There were rumors of me leaving, but the club members insisted the gift of a car wasn't meant to keep me at William and Mary. They said it was a reward for the good things I had already done.

It wouldn't be right for me to keep the car when I knew I was probably going to agree to take the coaching job at NC State very soon. I told them I could not accept the car, but I appreciated their sentiments very much.

After our last game on Saturday, I knew we were headed to Raleigh, North Carolina, the very next day to reach a final decision about whether or not to accept the NC State job. My wife greeted me when I came home and said, "Honey, you won't believe what happened today at the game. At halftime someone called me out of the stands and gave me the keys to a new car!"

"We can't keep that car," I said immediately.

"Well, they gave it to *me*, and we won't make it to Raleigh in our old car."

I called the president of the Quarterback Club that night and tried to give the car back again. He refused, so off we drove to North Carolina State the next day in the car that William and Mary gave my wife.

We accepted the job at NC State, were there for four years, and went to four straight bowl games. We were very, very successful. Coaching at North Carolina State was a great experience and benefit to my career. Raleigh was a wonderful place to live.

The point is that when you do the right thing—even if it seems it may cause you to lose out on something you really want—in the long run you will never regret it. I still must admit, though, it was wrong for us to take that car when we knew we were leaving. But then again, it was my wife's decision.

Sacrifice and Self-Discipline

To do what is right on a daily basis does take sacrifice and self-discipline in order for this part of your plan to be successful.

It's also right to always be on time.

When I started coaching at Notre Dame, the team was coming off a season-ending loss to Miami, 58–7. Morale on the team wasn't very high. I walked into the staff room with my new assistants and said, "You know we are going to have to win early because Notre Dame isn't real patient."

That meant hard work and sacrifice. But we had problems right away. All the players complained because they had to lift weights, they had to work out, and they had to practice hard. We were determined not to accept anything less, but they still complained.

Photo by Focus on Sport/Getty Images

This is what happens when you are losing. You complain about how much work you have. You're going to find a hundred things to complain about on a continuous basis.

Related to the sacrifice it takes to succeed is self-discipline. And remember: Discipline is not what you do *to* somebody. Discipline is what you do *for* somebody.

As a coach, I never really disciplined people. People always bring up the time I sent our leading ground gainer and our leading receiver home from Los Angeles before the 1988 Notre Dame–Southern Cal game because they were late for a team meal. This was the final game of the regular season, a game between the number-one- and number-two-ranked teams in the nation.

That really did happen. But it wasn't my choice to send them home. It was the players' choice. All I did was to enforce their decision. They had been late before, and I told them: "If you do this one more time—your fault, my fault, the bus driver's fault, heart attack, I don't care—you are choosing not to play in the game."

Remember: discipline is not what you do *to* somebody. Discipline is what you do *for* somebody.

They chose to violate the team rules. They were late again. I didn't discipline them. I enforced their decision. Abiding by the rules of those in authority in your lives—your employer, military superior, or your religious leader—requires self-discipline.

Keep a Positive Attitude

Doing the right thing on a daily basis is difficult, no doubt about it. But that doesn't give you permission to be bitter and spread a nasty attitude toward others. No employer, no spouse, and no friend wants to constantly be dragged down by your bitterness.

Everyone has injustices done to them: by society, by a professor, or by an employer. You have to be careful. You don't want to go through life being so bitter that when you pass away your spouse has to hire six pall-bearers to carry your coffin because you don't have any friends left.

You are going to have problems and difficulties. That's part of life. Just because you've graduated and you're done writing papers, taking exams, and dealing with uncooperative people on campus doesn't mean you aren't going to have new problems in the future. They key is to not let your problems take over your attitude. Here are two suggestions: Don't let your problems make you bitter. Also, don't tell anyone your problems. Do you know that 90 percent of people don't care about your problems? And the other 10 percent are glad you've got them.

There is never an easy way to handle your problems, but you can cope with them. On June 21, 2015, my wife and I were awakened at 2:30 a.m. by the smoke alarm, which told me our house was on fire.

We got outside with basically just our bathrobes and watched our house burn to the ground. Every possession we had was lost in the fire.

Here are two suggestions:
Don't let your problems make you bitter.
Also, don't tell anyone your problems.

But the thing was, we didn't lose anything in the fire that we were going to take with us to heaven. We both already knew that the only thing coming with us to heaven is our children.

By 8:00 a.m. the reality of the situation had set in. There was nothing left on our property but smoldering ashes. My wife stood by me crying. I said to her, "We have twenty-four hours to cry and feel sorry for ourselves. But come 8:00 a.m. tomorrow, we are never going to look back. We are going to build this house bigger and better, and we are never going to ask *what if* or *why*."

That was the attitude we took. I gave my wife an unlimited budget to rebuild the house, and she exceeded it. But I can assure you that she built a much better house than the one we had lost. As a matter of fact, just recently, she surprised me and said, "Our house burning down turned out to be a very positive thing for us." I completely agree with her.

In order to have an excellent, positive attitude even in the midst of problems and difficulties, you need to enjoy life and have fun. I'm guessing you had fun while you were in school. You don't need to stop having fun now that you are beginning your professional career.

Cal Sport Media via AP Images

Have fun with what you are doing. People always ask me if I had fun doing the *College GameDay* show on ESPN. I tell them "not really." I was up there in Bristol, Connecticut, which was fifteen minutes from Hartford by telephone. And I'm on the set with a guy named Mark May. Now I love Mark May. Mark is a beautiful guy. But we had a difference of opinion.

He was a player. I was a coach.

He made suggestions. I made decisions.

He showered after work. I showered before work.

He signed a paycheck on the back. I signed it on the front.

But you know what, in spite of all that, when they turned on the red light and we went on live television, I was going to have fun with Mark May. When you have fun doing something, people have fun being around you. When you have fun at what you are doing, it's a lot easier to keep an excellent, positive attitude.

Every day when I walked out onto the football field, the first thing I said was "what a great day to work." And I meant it.

Don't Let Other People Tear You Down

What is to prevent you from doing the right thing? What is to prevent you from always keeping a positive attitude? What is to prevent you from becoming bitter? A lot of the times it's the people around you that will drag you down. But that's only if you let them.

I coached at the University of Arkansas for seven years from 1977 to 1983. During those seven seasons we went to six bowl games, had four top ten finishes, had the best winning percentage in the history of the school, and had the second best winning percentage in the history of the Southwest Conference. We filled the stadium. The players on those teams graduated. We ran an honest program.

To show their appreciation, the athletic director, Frank Broyles, fired me. When I asked him why, he said it was for the "betterment of the program" and that he would not give me a reason. I was so mad and upset I wanted to go to the media and tell my side of the story. I knew where all the bodies were buried,

AP Photo/Phil Sandlin, File

and I wanted to blast everybody at the University of Arkansas. My wife told me, "No, don't do that. We know what we accomplished here. We will move on." We never held a press conference, and I never said a negative word. I went on to coach at the University of Minnesota.

Two years later, in 1985, Gene Corrigan, the athletic director at Notre Dame, called Frank Broyles and told him that he was looking at several coaches for the Notre Dame job. He wondered what had happened to Lou Holtz.

19

Frank Boyles admitted to Gene Corrigan than he had taken the word of somebody who had told him something about me that was not true. He told Gene Corrigan that I was the best coach he had ever been around and that he knew for a fact I had always wanted to coach at Notre Dame. He said, "Don't talk to anyone else. If you can hire Lou Holtz at Notre Dame, you will never regret it."

So the person who fired me ended up giving me the highest recommendation for the job I always wanted: to be the head coach at the University of Notre Dame.

Let me tell you another story about the importance of not letting other people tear you down. Many years ago Notre Dame was scheduled to play on New Year's Day against the University of Florida in the Sugar Bowl. I felt Notre Dame would play very well. I sent our football team away for two days at Christmas to spend time with their families. I've always believed that is important to do around the holidays. My wife and children and I gathered in Orlando to spend time with our own family.

We have four children, and they're all girls but two, and I'm very proud of them. I am never happier when I am with my family. We were sitting in a restaurant and the waiter recognized me and came over. He said, "You're Lou Holtz, the coach of Notre Dame, aren't you?"

I said, "Yes, sir," and I took out my pen because I thought he wanted my autograph.

He waved me off and said, "I've got a question, Coach. What is the difference between Notre Dame and Cheerios?"

I said, "I have no idea."

He said, "Cheerios belong in a bowl, and Notre Dame doesn't."

This is a true story. Well, my attitude changed. My wife noticed right away. She told me, "Are you going to let a perfect stranger put you in a bad mood and ruin a night out with your family?"

She was right. I couldn't let what this one individual said to me change what had been my positive attitude to a negative one. I couldn't let what he said ruin the night with the people I love the most.

I shrugged off what he said, and we enjoyed a fine meal.

When it was time for the check, I called the waiter back over. I looked at him and said, "Now, let me ask you a question. What is the difference between Lou Holtz and a golf pro?"

The main shook his head and said he didn't know.

I said, "A golf pro gives tips."

Keep Your Commitments

In your days in school, you probably participated in an extracurricular activity. Maybe it was sports, a language club, or the band. When you signed up, your parents may have told you something like, "If you start with this activity and make a commitment to it, you have to honor the commitment." For my wife and I, this was the message to our kids. We expected them to keep their commitments whether or not they liked the coach, whether or not they won or lost, and whether they played or sat on the bench. Quitting during the season would be the easy way out and would not be an option.

Making and keeping commitments will continue to be a big part of your life. There are different kinds of commitments for adults. A marriage commitment is permanent commitment and will be in place for your entire life. This means that when you are getting serious about someone you might marry, you should ask yourself questions such as these:

- How does this person treat me?
- How does this person treat others?
- Is this person someone I will be proud to marry in front of my family and friends?
- Is this person someone with whom I want to have and raise children?

In making this type of commitment, you shouldn't have to settle for anything but the best.

Commitment is also important on your job. You should honor your initial commitment you make to an employer. The employer is making a commitment to you. You were hired, weren't you? You must keep your commitment to the employer by following the regulations of the company, participating in the proper training, and doing the correct job in the manner that fits the company's requirements and your skills.

Making and keeping commitments will continue to be a big part of your life.

However, if you feel the job is not for you after your initial commitment is up (the actual time for the initial commitment varies from job to job), then make a reasoned decision and move on to something else. If this does happen to you on a job and you are faced with this type of a decision, go back to the basic questions: "What am I trying to do?" and, especially, "What is the right thing to do?"

DO EVERYTHING TO THE BEST OF YOUR ABILITY

I was born with a silver spoon in my mouth. I have been very fortunate throughout my life.

I was born on January 6, 1937, during the Depression, in Follansbee, West Virginia, a city of fewer than three thousand people along the Ohio River.

I was born in the cellar at home, delivered by a Dr. McGraw.

We had one bedroom for my parents, my sister, and me. I do not recall us even having a closet in that bedroom, but then again, we didn't really need one. I only had one pair of pants.

We had a kitchen and a half bath. That half bath did not have a tub, a shower, or a sink.

For seven and a half years we lived in that house. There was no welfare or food stamps at the time. There were no government safety nets at all. But I always had plenty to eat. I know this because every time I asked for seconds my dad would say, "No, you had plenty."

The reason I say that I was born with a silver spoon in my mouth is because I was born in this country, the United States of America, and I was taught that if I was willing to get an education, make good choices, work hard, and utilize the talents God gave me, then I could have a happy and successful life.

I was not unplanned. I was part of God's plan, and God had a plan for me.

I was not unwanted. God created me. My parents welcomed me.

I was not unloved. God loved me, and my parents loved me very much.

We did not have many material possessions in our home in Follansbee, West Virginia. But it's not what you have material-wise that determines whether or not you are born with a silver spoon in your mouth.

More importantly, the blessings come from being planned, wanted, and loved. I was all of those things. I was blessed in those respects. I have been very fortunate in my life.

I was not unplanned. I was part of God's plan, and God had a plan for me.

I am assuming by your circumstances in reading this book that you have been very blessed too. With our blessings come responsibilities. These responsibilities form the heart of the second rule for living a good life: do everything to the best of your ability.

Making Choices in Life

The two most important days in your life, as Mark Twain once said, are the day you were born and the day you discover *why* you were born.

Everything I have learned from all my years on this earth is centered on the fact that we can't accomplish anything of worth by ourselves. We have to get along with other people and be able to work with other people. And taking it one step further, we have to help people in need. We were born for these reasons.

All of these lessons definitely apply in business and your work life.

Every business, according to Zig Ziglar, a prolific American salesperson, is predicated upon finding out what the customers want and showing them how you can help them get what they want better than anyone else can. This is the basis of most professions and jobs in a consumer society, and it usually requires everyone in the company cooperating with both coworkers and customers and helping both coworkers and customers as needed.

It's one thing to understand these important lessons; it's another thing to put them into practice. I want to tell you that there are approximately four hundred thousand words in the English language. I didn't count them all, but I'm taking somebody's word for it. By far the most important word of all those is the word *choice*.

You have to make the *choice* to get along with others.

You have to make the *choice* to help others when called upon.

Remember the Golden Rule: "Do to others whatever you would have them do to you." You have to make the *choice* about whether or not you will keep it.

Whether you are successful or not in this life, whether your life is ultimately good or bad, is all because of the choices you make. Choose to do drugs, choose to drop out of school or the workforce, choose to abuse others, or choose other negative things, and there is a strong likelihood you have also chosen to have a difficult life. Bad choices alienate us and keep us alone and apart from others.

That's a difference between making a good choice and making a bad choice. A good choice usually brings us into contact with others and helps us to work together to succeed.

Obligations and Responsibilities to Yourself and Others

Not everyone can be an all-American. Not everyone can be on the first team. But everyone can be the best that they are capable of being and do everything to the best of their ability.

Now, if you want to fail, you have the right to fail. That's one of the great things about this country. It is your choice to fail or not. However, you do not have the right to cause others to fail because you are not doing everything to the best of your ability. When you marry a spouse, when you bring a child into the world, when you join a business, or when you join the military, you have obligations and responsibilities and you owe it to other people to do the maximum you can in everything you do.

Consider what happened to Jerome Bettis, one of the greatest running backs to ever play football, in the middle of his career.

Jerome played for me at the University of Notre Dame. After Notre Dame he went to the Los Angeles Rams and became the NFL rookie of the year. His

Photo by Joseph Patronite/Getty Images

second year in the pros Jerome wasn't very good. The third year everybody said he was washed up.

I watched the Rams play on TV that year, and Jerome did not play very well. I called him on the phone and said, "Jerome, this is Coach Holtz. I watched the Rams play, and there's some guy impersonating you, wearing your jersey and your number, and giving you a bad name. You gotta put a stop to it."

As soon as the season was over, Jerome made a series of good choices.

First, he showed up at my office. He said, "Coach, when I left Notre Dame I had a wonderful attitude. I went to the pros, and I let my attitude go down. I'm coming back to Notre Dame. And I'm going to spend the next four months getting my attitude right."

And that's what he did. He spent the summer at Notre Dame working out both on his own and with others. He rededicated himself to being the best football player he could be.

It just so happened, that in that off-season, Jerome was traded to the Pittsburgh Steelers. He became known as "the Bus," the league leader in rushing and eventually only the fourteenth player to rush for more than ten thousand yards in his career. The Steelers did not get the same player who played the year before with the Rams.

Jerome made the choice to be the best he could be. Same talent. Different attitude. Different results.

Remember: It Is Your Decision

Doing everything to the best of your ability is not an automatic function. It doesn't happen by magic. Everybody is looking for instant success, but it doesn't work that way. You build a successful life one day at a time. You build a successful life one choice at a time. There are many temptations along the way that can keep you from doing your best.

You alone have the freedom to choose between good and bad. This freedom is one of God's greatest gifts.

I think back to my early years in coaching, in the late 1960s. I coached with a man named Woody Hayes at Ohio State. Woody Hayes was one of the greatest

---

You alone have the freedom to choose between good and bad. This freedom is one of God's greatest gifts.

---

coaches of all time. When we played Purdue in 1968, they were ranked number one in the nation. We beat them that day.

I was really excited—not only because we had won the game versus the number one team but also because many of my relatives were at the game. All of my high school friends and fraternity buddies were there as well. We planned to party after the game well into the night.

But Coach Hayes had other ideas. He told all of his assistants to meet in the staff room at seven o'clock. It was Saturday night. I wanted to go out with my friends and celebrate. Coach Hayes wanted to begin preparations for the next opponent. I had a choice to make.

We prepared that night as a staff for the next opponent and went on to win. That year we won the national championship. Woody Hayes demanded sacrifice and self-discipline. He set before us a series of choices we had to make if we were to be the best we were going to be.

AP Photo/Gene Herrick

When you make choices that lead you to do something to the best of your ability, you are truly committed to excellence in your life.

———

SHOW PEOPLE THAT YOU CARE

When you walk into a room your attitude should not be "Hey, here I am; look at me!" No, your attitude should be "Here I am; how can I help you?" This is the way you can show people that you care, the third rule for living a good life.

My wife, Beth, is a stage-four cancer survivor. When her weight went from 129 pounds to 89 pounds, they gave her a 10 percent chance to live. I am happy

AP Photo/Joe Raymond

to report that my wife beat those odds and is doing well. I don't even pray for her any more. I pray *to* her.

We are opposites, my wife and I. She says opposites attract, then attack. She left me a note a couple of months ago that said, "Lou, I can't please everyone so I am going to stop trying. I'm going to focus on pleasing one person a day. Today is not your day, and tomorrow is not looking real promising either."

But Beth is really my best friend. We've been married nearly fifty-eight years. She never does interviews. She did do one interview in her life because I asked her to, and it was only to answer one question: "What did you learn from having cancer?"

She answered, "I learned how much my family loved me."

Now, we didn't love her any more after she got sick than we did before.

Why does someone have to go through something such as cancer before they realize how important they are to us?

Everyone you are going to meet the rest of your life needs a smile or a kind word. It's such a simple thing to give someone encouragement each day and to show you care. Make a promise to yourself that you will show people you care about them beginning today.

Overcoming Evil with Commitment, Forgiveness, and Respect

In fact, I used to be insanely jealous of my wife. She is so beautiful and talented. We would go to a cocktail party, and when I would see her talking with other men who were always better built, better looking, and more intelligent than me, I would get jealous. I would constantly ask myself, "Why wouldn't she rather be with him than me?"

This was entirely my problem. I was so insecure. And because of this lack of self-confidence, I would constantly criticize my wife and pull her self-confidence down to my level to where I thought she would then think she was lucky to have me as a husband.

I was absolutely wrong to do this. The union between people, and especially between a husband and wife, has always been threatened by the evil we experience around us and within ourselves. The evil often shows itself in things such as abuse, domination, and infidelity, besides jealousy. If these feelings are not brought into check, they can lead to hatred and separation.

You may find yourself behaving in a similar way now with a friend or a coworker or with someone you are dating. You can never completely overcome evil while living on earth, but you can try to do so by showing people you care through daily encouragement and signs of your love. The opposite of domination, infidelity, and jealousy is a caring and loving relationship, which is characterized by several related qualities, including the following:

- **Commitment.** When you care for and love another, you are able to weather the ups and downs of disagreements, tragedies, and other challenges in order to survive. Also, it takes great patience to truly know another person, accept them for who they are with all of their own faults, and then still be willing to commit to them over a lifetime.

- **Forgiveness.** When you care for and love another, you not only accept the other person for his or her faults but also forgive the other person in order to strengthen the relationship. You are always willing to say, "I am sorry. Please forgive me."

- **Respect.** When you care for and love another, you respect the other person and encourage the other person to reach his or her full potential.

Showing people you care builds trust. My wife and I have had a long marriage. Through the daily ways we care for one another, the trust between us has grown.

Trust and Caring Go Hand in Hand

Without trust, nothing you do really has a good chance for success. You build trust by caring for others.

This was certainly the case when I first came to coach football at the University of South Carolina. It was obvious that we did not have a great deal of trust on our team. I felt it was primarily because the players did not trust me. I had never had a problem like that before. Even after eighteen months on the job, I could tell the players still lacked trust. I just wasn't sure where this lack of trust was rooted.

We had a team meeting at the end of June after a discipline problem arose. The players knew about the problem and had not told me about it. Had they trusted me enough, I could have resolved the problem before it became national news. Now I wanted to know why they did not trust me enough to tell me what was going on.

At first, nobody said a word.

The longer their silence extended, the more frustrated I became.

Finally, one young man got up and spoke. "I do trust you, Coach. I think most of the players in this room trust you and the assistant coaches. But I don't trust many of my teammates in this room. Many of them lie."

He then proceeded to list a variety of other offenses his teammates had committed. When he sat down, some other players got up and expressed the same feelings he had.

As a result of that team meeting we came up with a list of covenants, or agreements, that our football team would live by. For example, players made an agreement that they were going to do things right, and that they would no longer sit by and watch one of their teammates do things that would jeopardize the team's chances for success.

I then passed out a blank sheet of paper to every member of the team. I asked them to write down all the things they did not like about themselves. After some time in silence, I told them to take those papers home and think about what they had written. In four-teen hours, we would meet again, and they would bring their papers along with them.

When they returned, we gathered up all the pa-pers without reading them. We took them to the field, put them in a pile, and burned them. We then dug a hole and buried the ashes.

I explained to our team that whatever they did not like about themselves was now in the past. They were going to start a brand-new life from that point on. All the mistrust and wrong decisions they had made in the past were over. And we now had agreements that we intended to live by.

I told them that the coaches and I would expect to see a different group of young men, a different group of students, and a different team from that point on. We expected to see a more caring group of players.

When this meeting ended, we put a small monument about three feet high over the place on the practice field where we buried the ashes. We didn't put any words on the monument—we didn't need to—because the players knew what was under there. They also knew that the experience of burying their mistakes and dislikes changed their lives and changed the team.

Any time you have a successful team in sports, I promise you it's because the players trust the coach and the coach trusts the players. Without trust, there is no chance for a relationship. Without trust, you don't have a chance at all to succeed.

What Happens When Enough People Care

What's the easiest way to get people to care about a team, an organization, or a place of business? Suffice to say, you won't be browbeaten into caring. No one can make you care. The easiest way to be a caring member of the group is to feel a stake in the group and to be truly involved.

A great deal of the responsibility for how much a player cares about the team rests on the shoulders of the coach. A great deal of the responsibility for how much an employee feels involved in the company and cares for the company's success rests on the supervisor and employer. But these people in positions of leadership can ultimately do only so much in creating a caring and successful group. It is also your responsibility to forge camaraderie with others. It is your responsibility to take pride in your work and in the group you belong to.

Your own attitude matters in whatever you do. Put yourself in the shoes of an employer or potential employer, and think about the kind of person he or she would want to hire and keep on the job.

I am reminded of the story of the foreman who made his rounds through the site where three workers were laying bricks for a great cathedral.

The easiest way to be a caring member of the group is to feel a stake in the group and to be truly involved.

The foreman asked the first worker, "What are you doing?" The first worker responded, "I'm making $9.95 an hour."

The foreman asked the second worker, "What are you doing?" The second worker said, "I'm laying brick until quitting time."

The foreman asked the same question of the third worker. "What are you doing?"

The third individual looked up from his work and said, "I am building the most beautiful cathedral this world has ever seen. And years from now people will have the opportunity to come and worship here and marvel at our commitment to excellence."

I ask you, if you were an employer, which of these bricklayers would you hire? Which would you want to be a part of your organization?

How can you be more like the person who cares the most about the nature of the job?

Another way to foster a caring environment in the workplace is to air any problem you might be having with your supervisor or coworkers in an appropriate manner. Why? Getting the problem off your chest will help you discover a very important lesson about those in leadership and your colleagues. The lesson is this: there are many people who care about you and who want to help you to solve the problem.

Similarly, this type of openness will make it more possible for someone else to come to you with a problem they are having or simply to engage you in friendly conversation. This openness goes hand in hand with trust. Remember, if my South Carolina team would have trusted one another all along, we might not have had some larger problems fester and spill out into the open. The coaches might not have had to gather the team as a group and have them secretly record their issues and grievances if the players would have trusted one another more in the first place and been willing and able to work their problems out on their own.

Whenever you are in a relationship with others, there is a good chance that you can help solve a problem someone else brings to you. You can certainly listen to this person share the problem. And I have found that when you listen to a person and possibly act to help solve the problem, this action will help you even more than it will help them. By being responsible and caring in this way, you will have more of a stake in the relationship. Airing your problems with a friend, a coworker, or a spouse in an appropriate way or helping these people to solve their problems will deepen the trust between you. It is a way to be caring.

Also, did you ever notice that on a company-wide scale, most of the large and successful businesses are usually heavily involved in charity work around the community? The reason is that the whole attitude of a successful business is to care for their customers. This care extends into other needs in the community. If you are personally going to be successful in your career, begin to foster this attitude in your own personal life. You will see the dividends.

You can certainly listen to a person share their problem. And I have found that when you listen to a person and possibly act to help solve the problem, this action will help you even more than it will help them.

As for me, I've received several recognitions in my life. They are never for what I did. They are for what other people around me have done for me and with me. I share these honors with my assistant coaches.

With my players. With my colleagues on television and radio. With my children. With my wife, Beth.

Whenever you receive recognition, pass the credit. No one succeeds alone. You've probably watched a Heisman Trophy presentation at the end of the college football season. The player who wins the award never gives an acceptance speech filled with long lists of his personal statistics and accomplishments. No, he makes sure to thank his parents, his high school coaches, his college coaches, the trainers and medical staff, his teammates, and God.

AP Photo/Ron Frehm

Sharing credit and recognition for a personal honor that was only accomplished with the help of many others is proper and builds a sense of care and trust among everyone involved.

Becoming More Trustworthy and Caring

When someone trusts you, they respect you, and when they respect you, you will respect yourself.

To be successful in life, people have to trust you. You might wonder, "How can I trust? How can I get people to trust me?" These are certainly crucial questions as you begin new relationships with coworkers, employers, and customers while trying to grow your relationships with family and friends.

The simple answer is to follow the three rules outlined in this book: Do what is right. Do everything to the best of your ability. Show people you care.

You can also try this exercise. Think about two people in your life. Pick one person you love, admire, and respect. Pick a second person you have some kind of problem with. Ask these three questions to yourself about both people. Answer with a simple yes or no.

The first question is "Can I trust you?"

The second question is "Are you committed to excellence?"

The last question is "Do you care about me?"

To be successful in life,
people have to trust you.

I guarantee that the person you admire and respect said yes to all three questions. Now, with the person you have a problem with, you've pinpointed why you have the problem: you can't trust them, they are not committed to excellence, or they don't care.

What about you? How can you be more trustworthy and caring?

I was the head football coach at Notre Dame and spent many great afternoons in Notre Dame Stadium. But do you know what event in the stadium I remember most? I remember the time that the Special Olympics were held in the stadium. Six thousand Special Olympians—people with disabilities who have many reasons to be bitter and negative—competed in games over the course of several days. Yet all that they wanted to do was be like everyone else. Compete and have fun. And love and be loved.

The first question is "Can I trust you?"
The second question is "Are you committed to excellence?"
The last question is "Do you care about me?"

You know what I did at the Special Olympics? I was a hugger. I had lane three. My only job was to run up and hug whoever finished that race—first, last, or in between—in lane three. That and say to the person, "I am proud of you."

You will never find a person who doesn't need encouragement.

You will never find a person who doesn't need you to show him or her a smile.

This is because everybody you meet has a problem. This includes your friends, parents, spouses, neighbors, coworkers, and employers.

They may have a sick child, a sick in-law, or a sick wife.

They may have financial problems.

They may have a relative getting ready to go to jail.

You don't know.

Let me tell you how one of my teams learned this lesson.

Most colleges and universities, including the ones I have coached at, have an intra-squad game to end spring practice. Years ago we would reward the winning team with a postgame steak dinner. The losers had to eat hot dogs and beans. We ended this tradition when I found out most of the players would rather eat hot dogs, hamburgers, and baked beans than steak.

So we chose another way to reward the "losers" for their inability to succeed in the spring game. Over the years, we have had those players do things such as donate blood to the American Red Cross, sponsor a charity, wash cars, clean up litter on the highway, and so on.

You will never find a person who doesn't need encouragement.
You will never find a person who doesn't need you to show him or her a smile.

What impressed me most was what followed in the aftermath of these one-time spring charity events. The teams took it upon themselves do more community service throughout the summer months and into the season. Our players over the years obviously came from good, solid families who had given them outstanding training. There was rarely a week that went by when I did not receive a letter from someone in the community, from a grade school, or from a charitable organization commending several of our players for their service. In those cases, the players did all of this good work without any fanfare. I can assure you that nobody on our staff even knew they were involved in these particular endeavors. They did it all on their own.

You Can Repay Others with Your Care

I hope you realize that there have been some very special people in your own life who have helped you immeasurably. You may not have understood how much these special people cared for you at the time, but now you only wish you could say thanks and repay them. Sometimes you may think it is not possible.

Let me tell you, you can repay them. You can repay those people who did so many outstanding things for you and helped you to accomplish so much by passing their care on to another person. You can show the same care they had for you to someone else.

When you "pass it on" in this way, don't expect anything in return—any compensation, publicity, or praise. Just do it because other people have helped you in the same way in the past.

The need is there. I don't care if it's the president of the United States. I don't care if it's the sergeant of the platoon. I don't care if it's the CEO of the company. Everybody you meet is going to need some encouragement and some care.

You make yourself a more trustworthy and caring person each day by passing on your kindness and gratefulness to others.

Sometimes a feeling of guilt or unworthiness may keep you from caring for others. It is important to get over feeling guilty. There is not an individual alive, myself included, who has not done dumb things. We wish we hadn't done them. But you can't go through life with an albatross around your neck. All you need to do is say "I'm sorry" and make amends and move on. With the air cleared, you are much more able to love and care for others. What's more, your self-confidence and self-image are sure to grow when you are able to put feelings of guilt behind and leave yourself free to be a more valuable and caring part of an organization, team, or partnership.

Keeping in mind the implications of these questions will help you significantly.

If you do what is right, it answers the question "Can I trust you?"

When you always do everything to the best of your ability, it answers the question "Are you committed to excellence?"

You have already finished school. That is a great accomplishment. There is no doubt you will continue on and accomplish many more things in your life. You may make a lot of money. You may be significant. But that will not make you successful. Only when you care for others will you truly achieve success.

Show your friends you care. Show your parents you care. Show your employer and coworkers you care. There is no such thing as magic in this area— only simple, daily efforts.

DREAM AND SET GOALS

They put a statue of me outside of Notre Dame Stadium. I guess they needed a place for the pigeons to land. If you go there you will find three words on the statue: trust, love, and commitment.

Those are the three rules I had for my children and my teams. They represent the three rules I have shared with you in this book. I have no doubt that these rules will work for you in your life.

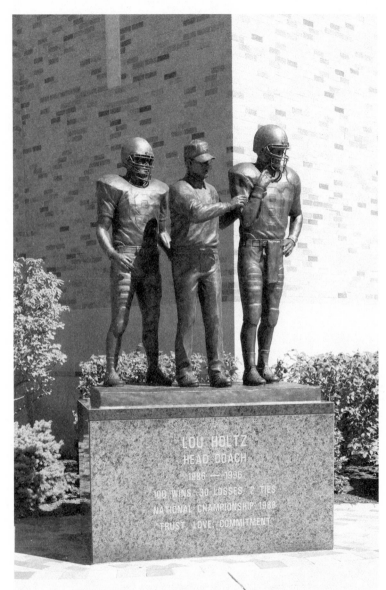

There is something else I want to share with you related to these rules: the importance of having a dream for your life and, to make your dream come true, the importance of having concrete goals.

My Path in Life

When I was young, I did not imagine the life I would eventually have. Since nobody in my family had ever gone to college, let alone graduated from college, I had no intentions whatsoever of doing so myself.

I was a very religious young man growing up. I was raised in a Catholic family. My initial goals in life were very humble. When I was a teenager, all I wanted was a car, a girl, a job in the mill, and five dollars in my wallet.

I played sports while I was in school and had various jobs. Finally I saved enough money to buy a 1949 Chevrolet. I thought that car was the greatest car in this world. However, before I could purchase the car, my high school coach, Wade Watts, came to our house and told my parents that he thought I should go to college. He thought I should study and train to become a coach.

I had no desire to go to college. But my parents listened to what Wade Watts told me. They said I should take all of the money I had saved for the 1949 Chevrolet and use it to pay for college. I said, "No, I am going to buy the Chevrolet." They said I was going to college, and so we compromised. I went to college. That was a typical compromise for my parents and me.

I went to Kent State University and ended up playing linebacker on the football team. I wasn't a particularly good football player. During the spring of my junior year, I sustained a knee injury. They did not do arthroscopic surgeries in those days. Knee surgeries were more complicated, and recovery time was much longer. I had to wait until the academic quarter ended in June before I could even have the surgery. It did not go well. I did not heal quickly enough for the start of my senior season. I would not be able to play. The coaches asked me if I would help coach the freshman football team and scout opposing teams on the weekends. I did both.

I graduated from Kent State in 1959 with a degree in history. I had been in the ROTC, and so I immediately went into the army. I imagined that when I got out of the service I would teach high school history, be an assistant high school football coach, and get married.

However, my college coach, Trevor Rees, had a buddy from his days in the navy named Forest Evashevski. Forest Evashevski was the head football coach at the University of Iowa. My coach prevailed upon Forest Evashevski to offer me a position as a graduate assistant coach. Those positions were not in vogue in those days. I would also be able to earn a master's degree if I went to Iowa.

So I had a choice to make: Do I go and get a master's degree from a prestigious university and learn more about football from a different coach, or do I stay in East Liverpool, teach in high school, and get married? That was an easy decision. I was going to be an assistant high school football coach and teach US history. And I was going to marry Beth Barcus.

The summer before school started—actually the exact date was July 9—Beth told me that she did not want to get married. She had a change of heart. She wanted to date her old boyfriend. I called my good friend Nevitt Stockdale that night. He shared his opinion that Beth and I had a love-hate relationship. He explained that I loved her and she hated me.

I wanted to get as far away from Beth as I possibly could, so at 10:30 that night Nevitt and I got in the car and drove straight through from East Liverpool, Ohio, to Iowa City, Iowa, with the hope that the graduate assistant job was still available. It was.

I had a fantastic year in Iowa. I learned so much from an outstanding staff. Our team finished second in the country.

Beth Barcus and I got back together after the season. We married on July 22, 1961. My first full-time position was as an assistant coach at the College of William and Mary.

I tell this story to explain how I got into college coaching instead of working at a mill or teaching and coaching at a high school.

> The point I want to make is
> that you should follow your heart.

I also think back to my East Liverpool High School coach Wade Watts who told my parents I should go to college and be a coach. If he had not told my parents that he thought I might make a good coach, I don't think I ever would have ever ended up with the life I've had. I do believe, however, that Wade Watts meant I should be a high school coach, not the coach at Notre Dame.

I guess I exceeded his expectations and my expectations too. The point I want to make is that you should follow your heart. When you accept advice from people who you trust and make good, right choices along the way, it can lead to something big.

The Importance of Goals

I cannot emphasize enough how important it is to have dreams and goals. From the previous story, I think you can see that I never had any well-planned career or life goals when I was young. When my first-grade teacher, Sister Mary Bernadette, asked the class what they wanted to be when they grew up, several children wanted to be lawyers and doctors. Others wanted to be police officers and fire fighters. I wanted to be a garbage collector. That shocked everyone, especially Sister Mary Bernadette. She asked me why. I said, "They only work on Tuesdays."

I changed. I grew up to understand how important it is to have dreams and goals. Dreams make things happen.

I first started naming my dreams when I was twenty-eight years old. And that's when I first started acting on my goals. Before that I just sort of went along with whatever happened to me.

This was in 1966 when I took a job at the University of South Carolina as an assistant coach under a head coach by the name of Marvin Bass. My wife was eight months pregnant with our third child, Kevin. I was only there about a month when I picked up the morning paper and read the headline: "Marvin Bass Resigns." I said to my wife, "I wonder if he's related to my coach."

Well, obviously they were one and the same, and the next thing you know I was unemployed. My wife had to go to work, and I stayed home. And I got this book that said that if you're bored with your life, if you don't have a burning desire for anything, you should name your dreams and write them down. I started really thinking about my life. What were the things I wanted to do? What did I what to accomplish?

I broke my dreams down into five categories:

1. Things I wanted to do religiously and spiritually
2. Things I wanted to do as a husband and father
3. Things I wanted to accomplish professionally
4. Things I wanted to accomplish financially
5. Things I wanted to do for excitement

Then I started to list all my goals in each of these categories:

- I wanted to parachute out of an airplane.
- I wanted to land on an aircraft carrier.
- I wanted to go whitewater rafting on the Snake River in Hells Canyon.
- I wanted to go in a submarine.
- I wanted to go to the White House for dinner.
- I wanted to see the pope.
- I wanted to visit the Holy Land.
- I wanted to go on an African safari.
- I wanted to go to Pamplona and run with the bulls (but with a person slower than me).

I wrote down all 107 of my goals. My wife came home from work, and I said to her, "Here are 107 of my goals. We are going to do them all."

She looked at them and said, "Gee, that's great. Why don't you go ahead and get a job."

So we made it a list of 108 instead.

What Are Your Goals?

In this day and age, you can't wait until you are in your late twenties to name your goals. In fact, I think you have to always have a plan about where you want to be one year from now in your personal life, religious life, and professional life. You need to have a goal about where you want to be financially in one year. And as I did, you need to include a category for what you want to do for excitement. Along with writing down these goals, you should make up some questions that go with them. You should include questions such as these:

- What financial price are you willing to pay in order to achieve these goals?
- What personal sacrifices are you willing to make?
- What bad habits do you have to get rid of in order to achieve your goals?
- Whom do you have to work with to achieve these goals? (Remember, you are not going to be able to achieve success without the help of others.)

- What problems and obstacles are you going to have to overcome? (Don't forget: everyone has them.)
- What is your plan to reach all of your goals?

I think having goals is very important. But what is more important is having a philosophy about your life and how you are going to live. The three rules I have cited in this book are the three rules I have tried to follow and live by for my entire adult life.

These three rules—do what is right, do everything to the best of your ability, and show people you care—have never let me down.

My Hope for You

I always told my children that when looking at your future, find something you love to do and something you are good at. They should be one and the same. And most importantly, find somebody to pay you to do it.

You might love to paint and you may do it pretty well. If you can find someone to buy your paintings, you could have a profession. If you don't find some-body to buy your paintings, you have a hobby.

I do believe that regardless of what you do from this point forward in both your career and your personal life, if you rise up and people respect you, if they know you are committed to excellence, and that you care for them and others, you will live a life in which you are richly rewarded.

I will pray for you and your success. I wish you all the best.

TEN GREAT LOU HOLTZ QUOTATIONS

1. Motivation is simple. Eliminate those who are not motivated.

2. If you're bored with life—you don't get up every morning with a burning desire to do things—you don't have enough goals.

3. You were not born a winner, and you were not born a loser. You are what you make yourself to be.

4. Everyone needs something to do, someone to love, something to hope for, and something to believe in.

5. One thing is certain: there will be one thing that will dominate your life. I strongly suggest it be something you can be proud of.

6. Ability is what you are capable of doing. Motivation determines what you do. Attitude determines how well you do it.

7. Without self-discipline, success is impossible. Period.

8. Virtually nothing is impossible in this world if you just put your mind to it and maintain a positive attitude.

9. Making a big life change is pretty scary. But you know what's even scarier? Regret.

10. I can't believe God put us on this earth to be ordinary.

AVE